Mata Ganga Ji and the Naulakha Necklace

Written by:
Prem Ras Books

Illustrated by:
Yevheniia Lisova

Dedicated to Guru Arjan Dev Ji, who blessed the world
with an eternal Naulakha Necklace.

Bhul Chuk Di Maafi Baksho

Published in association with
Bear With Us Productions

ISBN:

Cover by Richie Evans
Design by Tommaso Pigliapochi
Illustrated by Yevheniia Lisova

www.justbearwithus.com

Mata Ganga Ji and the Naulakha Necklace

Written by:

Prem Ras Books

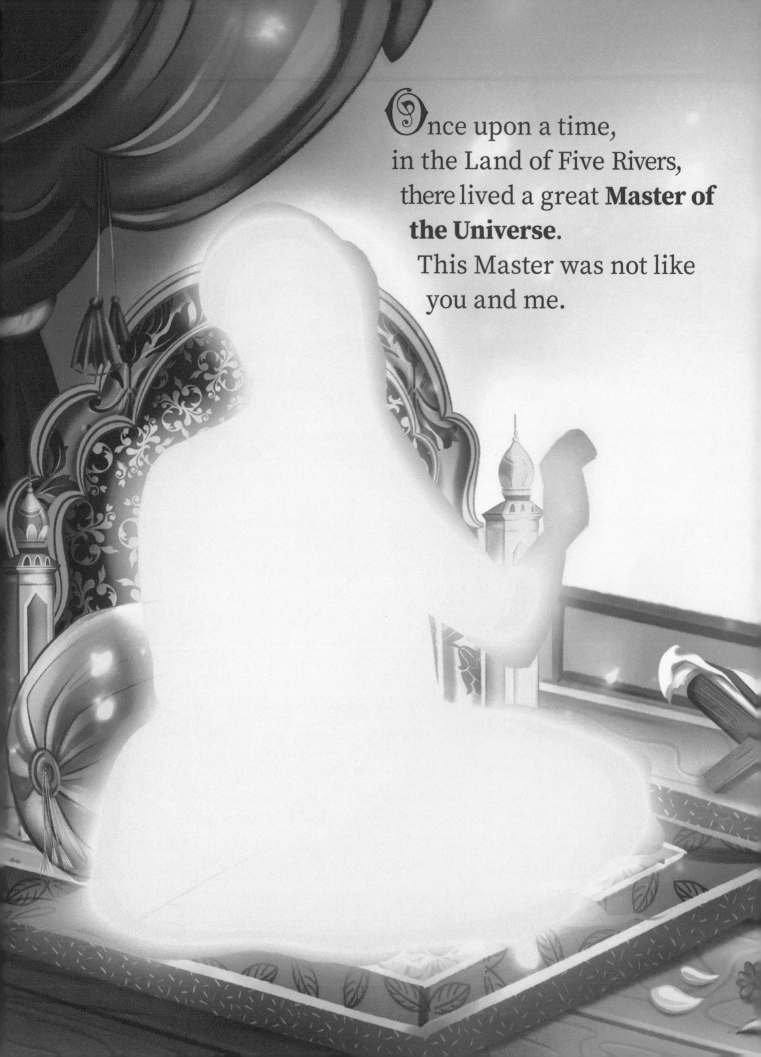

Once upon a time,
in the Land of Five Rivers,
there lived a great **Master of
the Universe**.
This Master was not like
you and me.

He could heal the sick with
the touch of his glance.

He could endure the heat of fire
and coal without a groan.

He could erect palaces made
from the dust of heaven.

His name was
Guru Arjan Dev Ji.
Maybe you have heard of him?

Guru Arjan Dev Ji also had a wife.
Her name was **Mata Ganga Ji**.

Mata Ganga Ji was very special, too. She had eyes that twinkled at the beauty surrounding her, and a heart that marvelled at the wonders of the world. She had ambition and determination, as well as innocence and joyfullness.

In those days, many people of significant stature would visit the Guru hoping to receive blessings. With their fancy, bejewelled clothes, proud gaits, and noses high in the air, folks of grand extravagance and wealth would arrive from far and wide at the Guru's gate to seek his spiritual gifts.

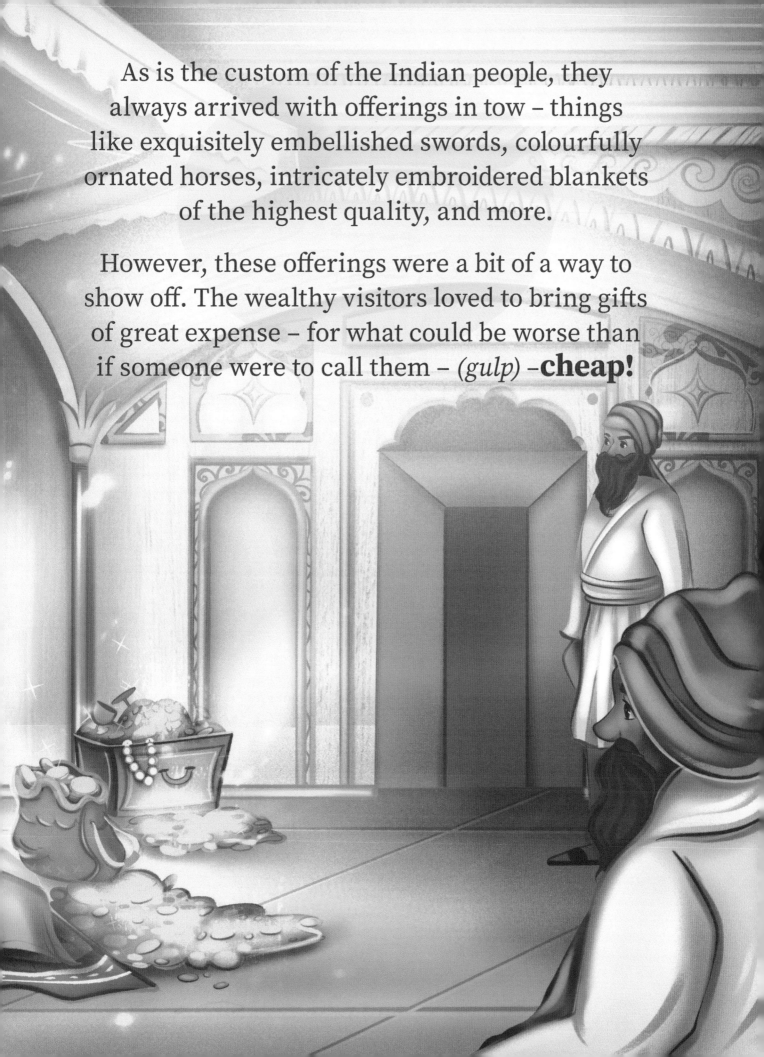

As is the custom of the Indian people, they always arrived with offerings in tow – things like exquisitely embellished swords, colourfully ornated horses, intricately embroidered blankets of the highest quality, and more.

However, these offerings were a bit of a way to show off. The wealthy visitors loved to bring gifts of great expense – for what could be worse than if someone were to call them – *(gulp)* –**cheap!**

Guru Arjan Dev Ji had warned Mata Ganga Ji about the prideful antics of the rich. His demeanour was simple and humble, and he was not impressed by the extravagance of one's gifts but rather by the richness of one's heart. One day, a wealthy man brought a stunning gift that had people talking all over the land.

It was a **Naulakha Necklace** – a necklace worth precisely 900 000 coins. It was quite a sight to see. Its sparkling pearls beaded together to form several long chains, dangling delicately from its golden threads. Rare diamonds were studded into its tortuously designed centrepiece, adorned with tiny, glistening gems and crystals.

When the princesses and noblewomen of the land heard of the necklace, many flocked excitedly to the Guru's temple in hopes of having a look for themselves. The Guru however, was hardly bothered by it, and did not wear it.

The princesses and noblewomen went to Mata Ganga Ji.

"Sister Ganga!" they exclaimed. *"Why are you not wearing the Naulakha Necklace that has so graciously been gifted to your husband?"*

"Me?" asked Mata Ganga Ji, surprised.

"Why should I be wearing it?"

"Oh, Sister, you are so innocent," cooed one of the women. *"Of course, you should be wearing it. You are the wife of the Master and the mother of the nation. Why should you wear such simple clothes when your status is not of a peasant, but of a Queen?"*

"And Sister," chimed another. *"It will look oh so glorious beneath your already beautiful face. People will look and be so inspired by your glamour."*

All the women surrounded the lotus-minded Mata Ganga Ji and urged her to convince Guru Arjan Dev Ji to let her wear the Naulakha Necklace.

Later that day, Mata Ganga Ji sat on her bed, contemplating their words. It certainly was a stunning necklace. She had never worn jewelry or had even thought to – for jewelry was only worn either by the very rich, or by impoverished slave women.

But this necklace had begun to intrigue her mind. Why shouldn't she be able to have it?

At that moment, Guru Arjan Dev Ji entered the room. Mata Ganga Ji's face fell into a pout, to which the Guru smiled, amused. *"Ganga,"* spoke the Guru. *"Has something caused you to be upset?"* At first, Mata Ganga Ji sighed and shrugged, but her words quickly began to spill out.

"Oh beloved husband, I have never even asked for anything before, you know me, but it seems such a waste for that generous gift of yours to be sitting, wasting away, with no one to wear it, and no one to see it, and I just really, really wanted to try it on once, and all of the princesses were saying it would look very nice on me...."

The Guru laughed. *"Oh, innocent one. I told you not to listen to those rich people. That necklace is of no use to us. Will it go with us when we leave this world? If not, why become attached to it?"* Mata Ganga Ji was disappointed.
She felt upset, as by now she had wished to wear it.

Sensing Mata Ganga Ji's disappointment, the Guru drew closer. At that moment, a glow appeared on Guru Arjan Dev Ji's face. He lifted a hand and touched it to Mata Ganga Ji's head.

Suddenly, Mata Ganga Ji felt her breath catch. The world around her darkened swiftly like the sun had dropped speedily into the horizon's abyss.
A strange sensation came over her as she fell into a trance. A very odd feeling of standing under a pleasant and sweet-tasting rainfall came over her, yet her clothes were not getting wet.

Even more oddly still, she could suddenly hear musical notes which she had never heard before, enter the room like honey bees, buzzing and whirring around her.
They were picking up some chorus, growing steadily louder and louder.

"**Ganga.**" Guru Arjan Dev Ji's voice resounded loudly, snapping her back to herself. It sounded as if his voice was coming from deep inside her. "*Would you still like to have a beautiful necklace?*" Mata Ganga Ji murmured robotically, still entranced: "*Yes, beloved husband.*"

"*Then let us thread you a necklace that will stay with you forever. A necklace with beauty the likes of which this world has never seen before.*"

At that moment, Guru Arjan Dev Ji closed his eyes. The pleasant rainfall turned into a torrent. It was as if the sky above had opened up to a storm of sticky sweetness, indescribable sounds, and... letters.

Yes - letters.

Curvy, swirly, squiggly, entrancing little letters. As Guru Arjan Dev Ji spoke, these letters began to enter the torrent like butterflies sucked into a tornado. Guru Arjan Dev Ji's melodious voice rang out above the chaos, and Mata Ganga Ji listened in complete astonishment as all of the divine wonders danced to the Master's voice.
A delightful thing began to happen.
As he sang, the letters started to join together, making words, verses, and stanzas, like beads hung upon an invisible string.
The letters were forming a necklace.

The necklace that Guru Arjan Dev Ji made:

*(The poetry that Guru Arjan Dev Ji spoke in those moments was called **"Baavan Akhri"** – which means "52 Letters."*

In this composition, the Guru uttered verses for every letter of the Gurmukhi alphabet, explaining life, goodness, and the path to the Almighty Creator who sits in every person's heart.

Here is a bit of his message below. This is NOT a full translation, but a summary of some of the main points given to the letters of the alphabet throughout the composition. Baavan Akhri is, in fact, much longer than this - and we don't have enough pages to cover all of it!)

ੳ – The Universal Creator created the universe through the Word.

ਅ – With divine letters, the worlds were made.

ੲ – The divine letters were strung upon His one thread.

ਸ – The Lord is true, true, true!

ਹ – Look! The Lord is in each and every heart.

ਕ – He is the Creator and the Cause.

ਖ – He is bountiful – He will always continue to give. He fills the empty souls over the brim.

ਗ – Immerse yourself in His glory with each and every breath.

ਘ – There is no one but the Lord.

ਙ – Wisdom is not gained by simply talking.

ਚ – Blessed is the day when I become attached to the Lord's Lotus Feet (inside my heart).

ਛ – Lord, I am your child, and I am also your servant.

ਜ – It is our ego that makes us believe that we are the ones that are doing things or causing things to happen in this world.

ਝ – Sorrows will disappear when you deal in the business of the Lord's Naam*.

ਞ – Know this to be true, that (worldly) love will one day come to an end.

ਟ – Work for the Lord, for no one returns empty-handed from Him.

ਠ – Those people who have given up on everything else and have clung to the One Lord alone do not make trouble for anyone else's mind.

ਡ – This is not your True home – you must understand where that place is.

ਢ – Where are you going, wandering, and searching? Search instead within your mind.

ਣ – One who conquers his self wins the battle of life.

ਤ – Love the Treasure of Virtues; the Lord of the Universe, our King.

ਥ – Nothing is permanent – why do you stretch out your feet? (Why do you act like you will be here forever?)

ਦ – The One Lord is the Great Giver; He is the Giver to all.

ਧ – The mind's wanderings stop when one comes to swell in the Society of Saints.

ਨ – Those whose minds and bodies are filled will the Naam of the Lord shall not fall into the Underworld.

ਪ – He cannot be measured or understood – His end cannot be found.

ਫ – After wandering and wandering, you have arrived in this world – you have obtained the human body, so very difficult to obtain. Don't let this opportunity slip from your fingers.

ਬ – One who knows the Lord is the (true) "Brahmin".

ਭ – Destroy your delusion – the world is just a dream.

ਮ – Those who understand the Lord's mystery stay content because they look at pleasure and pain as the same.

ਜ – Burn away evil-mindedness.

ਰ – Be the dust of the feet of all and give up your ego and pride.

ਲ – One who takes the medicine of the Naam of the Lord is cured of pain and sorrow.

ਵ – Do not hate anyone, for the Lord is in each and every heart.

ੜ – In holy company, all conflict is eliminated.

***Naam** means "name" - see Afternote.*

Mata Ganga Ji was unsure as to how long the song had gone on. It could have been days, and it may only have been minutes. As rapidly as it had begun, the song was now concluding.
The necklace was now complete.
She could feel all of the letters settling comfortably in some cozy place within her heart, embedding themselves inside of her, etching themselves into the walls of her soul. Even at the conclusion of the song, the rainfall of sweet nectar continued to wash over her. And in fact, from that day onwards, the rainfall never did stop. From that day on, Mata Ganga Ji lived life shining like an emerald pearl, even without the fancy Naulakha Necklace.

For, the lesson here is this:

The gift of true beauty that had been given to her – and to all of us – was worth more than any diamond or gold necklace in the whole wide world.

Afternote

What do the 52 Letters represent?

Well, they represent the entire universe. Because these letters are sound, energy, essence – the same sound, energy and essence that Naam is made of.

What is Naam?

Although **"Naam" means "Name"**, it is much more than that. Naam is the thread that weaves through our entire universe and is the fabric beneath every single thing we see. **Naam is the Creator Himself.**

If that seems like a lot to wrap your head around, don't worry – it's a lot for adults, too! But one thing we can understand is the crucial message that Guru Arjan Dev Ji left us when he sang the song of the 52 Letters (Baavan Akhri) into existence. And that is to remember the Almighty who lives within all of our hearts - the home of true beauty.

This story was a re-imagining of the Sakhi of how Sri Bavan Akhri was recited for the first time. The original source where we took our information from was a small little Sakhi, hidden away in the pages of the book Gurmat Gauratva, by Bhai Sahib Randhir Singh Ji.

Bhai Randhir Singh Ji was an incredible Gursikh whose life and writings have influenced countless lives over the past century. He was the only individual in the last century to have been honoured by all of the original Takhat Sahibs for the contributions and sacrifices he had made for the Sikh Panth, having demonstrated incredible religious steadfastness during the sixteen years he spent in prison in the name of righteousness. Some of Bhai Sahib's companions are still around today, and speak with glazed eyes about the spiritual aura and energy that followed him everywhere he'd go. Whatever he wrote, he experienced first-hand – diving into realms of divine experiences that the rest of us can only imagine. We are fortunate to have the privilege to bring this gem of a Sakhi, once nestled away in the dusty pages of one of Bhai Sahib's least-read books, to the fore. There are so many lessons that both children and adults can derive from it, and we hope that our retelling can do it just a little bit of justice. **May Guru Sahib forgive us for our mistakes.**

Below is a translation of the Sakhi written down by Bhai Randhir Singh Ji.

One time, Sri Guru Arjan Dev Ji, who is the knower of all, counselled his wife Mata Ganga Ji:

"Women of wealthy Mahajans and Khatris come see you daily, but regardless of how rich or polite they are, they still do not understand Gurmat. Do not be influenced by their Manmatt advice."

Saying this, Sri Guru Ji then left to go to Darbar.

That day, when Sri Guru Ji was preaching a sermon to the Sangat, an extremely wealthy Seth made an offering to the Guru: the naulakha necklace.

All of Amritsar Sahib was discussing this necklace. The wealthy women gathered to see the necklace and were infatuated by it.

Several of these women gathered to meet Mata Ganga Ji and began coaxing and asking her to wear the necklace, saying:

"You are the mother of this entire world but you are not even wearing any ornament. You are the queen of the world, yet you do not even have a necklace. As the wife of Sri Guru Arjan Dev Ji, it is not befitting that you do not have any decoration. Someone has presented the naulakha necklace before Sri Guru Arjan Dev Ji today. Being our Guru-Mata, and being the wife of Guru Arjan Dev Ji, it would only be becoming for you to wear that around your neck. We beseech you: please plead with Sri Guru Arjan Dev Ji to permit you to wear the necklace."

What else can be said; in this manner, the group of wealthy non-Sikh women managed to entice Mata Ganga Ji to wear the naulakha necklace.

Before Sri Guru Arjan Dev Ji arrived back at his residence from Darbar, Mata Ji lay down on her bed and pretended to be upset. All-knowing Satguru Ji understood the true reason behind Mata Ji's disposition and said, "Today you have been influenced by the 'Aanmat' teachings of the wealthy women who came to you today. I had warned you about this."

Sri Mata Ji came to attention at Guru Ji's arrival, and with folded hands, palla grasped before her, she beseeched, "Oh Sachay Patshah, this meek servant of yours has never asked you for anything. Today I am asking for one thing. Please be kind and grant me my wish."

Sri Guru Ji knew all, but still asked her, with sweet smile on his face, what her wish was. Sri Mata Ji replied, "Today a naulakha necklace was given as offering in your Darbar. Kindly permit me to wear your necklace."

Hearing this, Sri Guru Ji began to laugh and said:

"So you have confirmed that you came under the influence of the rich women who met you today. Oh innocent, naïve one: you are speaking of a necklace worth 900,000 rupees, but even if you wore necklaces worth millions and billions of rupees, it would still be a false and worthless thing for you to do. Today, we will make such a necklace for you that will not only help you in this world, but even in the next."

After saying these words, Sri Guru Arjan Dev Ji began to recite the Bani, Sri Bavan Akhri.

The divine and heavenly effect of this Bani was such that as Sri Mata Ji heard tit, it began to become engraved within her. Such a miraculous effect happened at this time that, upon hearing it, it became carved within Sri Mata Ji's beautiful heart and fully memorized. Having heard this beautiful Bani, Mata Ganga Ji's heart and soul were illuminated by the Bani. In this manner, Mata Ganga Ji wore the true naulakha necklace that was Sri Bavan Akhri.

Printed in Great Britain
by Amazon

44326647R00021